K

KINDERGARTEN

AGES 5–6

Writing

Learning Fun Workbook

Published by Highlights Learning • 815 Church Street • Honesdale, Pennsylvania 18431
ISBN: 978-1-68437-284-3
Mfg. 04/2020
Printed in Brainerd, MN, USA
First edition
10 9 8 7 6 5 4 3 2

For assistance in the preparation of this book, the editors would like to thank:
Vanessa Maldonado, MSEd; MS Literacy Ed. K–12; Reading/LA Consultant Cert.; K–5 Literacy Instructional Coach
Kristin Ward, MS Curriculum, Instruction, and Assessment; K–5 Mathematics Instructional Coach
Jump Start Press, Inc.

This Is Me!

My name is:

_____

- - - - - - - - - - - - - - - - - -

_____

_____

I live at:

_____

- - - - - - - - - - - - - - - - - -

_____

_____

- - - - - - - - - - - - - - - - - -

_____

I am this many years old:

_____

- - - - - - - - - - - - - - - - - -

_____

_____

My favorite color is:

_____

- - - - - - - - - - - - - - - - - -

_____

Draw a picture of yourself. Decorate the frame, too.

Circle all the letters in your name.

A B C D E F G H I
J K L M N O P Q
R S T U V W X Y Z

From A to Z

Alphabet: Uppercase Letters

Help Aaron and Alex find their goat, Zack. Trace the uppercase letters in order.

abc Daisies

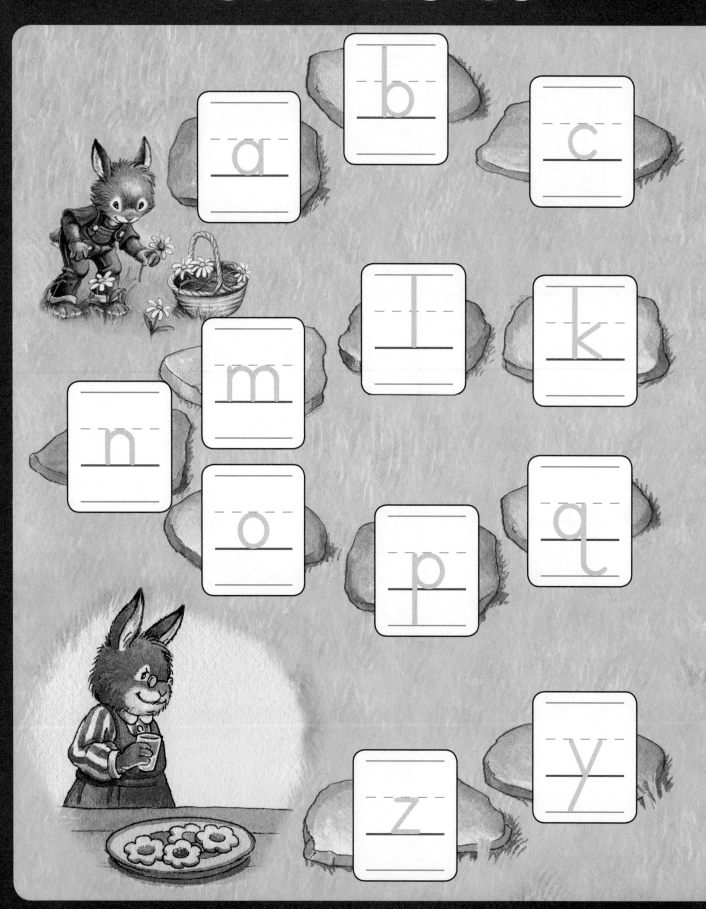

Little Bunny picked daisies for Mom, while Mom made daisy-shaped cookies for Little Bunny. Help Little Bunny find his way home by tracing the lowercase letters in order.

Head to Toe

Trace and say each word for a part of the body. Then write the word.

arm

ear

elbow

eye

foot

hair

hand

leg

Circle the differences you see between these pictures.

In these pictures, point to each body part listed on page 8.

9

Under the Rainbow

Trace and say each color word. Then write the word.

red

orange

yellow

green

blue

purple

pink

brown

Find **5** arrows in the picture. Color the arrows below to match.

What colors do you see in the picture?

Clowning Around

Trace and say each shape word. Then color the shape.

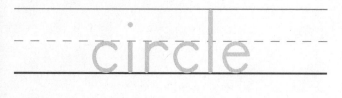 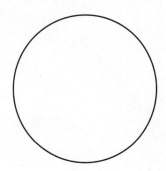

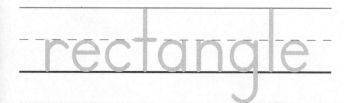 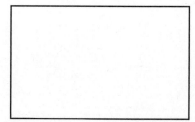

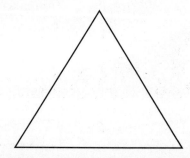

Can you find the **6** objects in this Hidden Pictures® puzzle?

What shapes do you see in this picture?

pizza

mug

bowling ball

stamp

slice of pie

pencil

13

Silly Garden

Trace and say each number and number word. Then write the number and number word.

1 one _____

2 two _____

3 three _____

4 four _____

5 five _____

6 six _____

7 seven _____

8 eight _____

How many of each item do you see in the picture?

What silly things do you see?

apples

orange carrots

birdhouses

pairs of sunglasses

squirrels

lollipops in a tree

people

Sled Ahead!

An **ordinal number** tells the order or position of something. Trace and say each ordinal word. Then write the word.

first

second

third

fourth

fifth

sixth

seventh

eighth

Follow each path to see who comes in first, second, and third.

Monkey See

Trace and say each word. Then write the word.

I **like** to go to the movies.

like

I **went** with Omar.

went

We **sat** in the second row.

sat

The movie **was** about a silly monkey.

was

Do you like **funny** movies?

funny

Circle the differences you see between these pictures.

A Good Day

Trace and say each word. Then write the word.

I **get** to class on time.

get

My teacher reads a poem to **us**.

us

He asks a question **about** it.

about

I raise **my** hand up high.

my

Who does the teacher **call** on?

call

Circle **10** pencils in the picture.

Barnyard Bagpipes

Trace and say each animal word. Then write the word.

The **cat** plays the bagpipes.

cat

The **cow** stops to listen.

cow

The **chicken** hugs her chicks.

chicken

The baby **pig** smiles at her mother.

pig

Does the **dog** like the music?

dog

Find the **8** objects in this Hidden Pictures® puzzle.

cake

needle

feather

mitten

star

purse

ruler

teacup

23

Lizzy's Busy Week

Trace and say each day-of-the-week word.

Monday

Tuesday

Wednesday

Thursday

Friday

Saturday

Sunday

Lizzy had a busy week. But the pictures here are all mixed up! Write 1, 2, 3, or 4 in each box to put her days in order. We did the first one to get you started.

SATURDAY

WEDNESDAY

FRIDAY

MONDAY

On the Job

Trace and say each question word. Then write the word.

Who is holding a hose?

Who

How does a doctor use a stethoscope?

How

When do you go to the library?

When

Where does your mail carrier leave letters?

Where

Why does a crossing guard wear orange?

Why

Draw a line to match each object to the person who needs it to do his or her job.

Puppet Show

Trace and say each word. Then write the word.

The snake is **above** the mouse.

above

The elephant is **below** the cat.

below

The white cat is **beside** the purple horse.

beside

A girl in pigtails is in **front** of the dog.

front

Who is **behind** the dragon?

behind

Circle the differences you see between these pictures.

Silly Campsite

Trace and say each word. Then write the word.

Tom's mom sits **on** a log.

on

Lisa lifts a burger **off** the grill.

off

Rashad plays **in** the camper.

in

Teddy takes a flashlight **out** of his pocket.

out

Which arrow points to the **left**?

left

Where Is Max's Hat?

Trace and say each word. Then write the word.

First, Max takes off his hat.

First

Next, he takes off his shoes.

Next

Then, Max steps into the water.

Then

After Max gets out, he looks for his hat.

After

Where did Max last see it?

last

Write **I**, **2**, **3**, or **4** to put these pictures in order. We did the first one to get you started.

Sweet Treats

Trace and say each word. Then write the word.

I **make** cookies with Mom.

make

I added **some** sugar.

some

Mom adds **more** flour.

more

We put the cookies in the oven.

_We_

Do you like to **help** make cookies?

help

Find the cookies in the picture. Color a cookie for each one you find.

Down Under

Trace and say each word. Then write the word.

Some animals live **under** the ground.

under

They must go **down** to go home.

down

Please help these meerkats!

Please

One **would** like to take a bath.

would

Who wants to read in a **big** chair?

big

Follow each path to see where each animal lives.

Superhero Party

Trace and say each word. Then write the word.

This birthday party is for Pilar.

This

She made capes for **all** her friends.

all

Each cape has a letter on it.

Each

What letter **does** Pilar wear?

does

How **many** candles are on her cake?

many

Find the **8** objects in this Hidden Pictures® puzzle.

wishbone

golf club

magnifying glass

toothbrush

pickle

caterpillar

wristwatch

slice of pie

My Favorite Book

Draw a picture from your favorite book. Then write the title of the book.

Writing: Opinion

Write to tell about the book.

This book is about . . .

_____

- - - - - - - - - - - - - - - - -

_____

- - - - - - - - - - - - - - - - -

_____

I like this book because . . .

- - - - - - - - - - - - - - - - -

_____

- - - - - - - - - - - - - - - - -

_____

My favorite part was when . . .

- - - - - - - - - - - - - - - - -

_____

- - - - - - - - - - - - - - - - -

_____

Make a Castle

Write about what you see in the picture. Here are some words you can use.

boxes   castle   dragon   knights

paint   paper   tape

This is a . . .

_____

_____

_____

It is made of . . .

_____

_____

_____

The kids are pretending . . .

_____

_____

_____

Can you find **5** hidden envelopes? Color an envelope below for each one you see.

Would you rather pretend to be a knight or a dragon? Why?

43

Silly Trip

What silly things do you see?

Writing: Narrative Text

Write some words or sentences to tell a silly story about what you see in this picture. Here are some words you can use.

away	car	duck	fish	kite
over	pie	pool	ride	truck

First I saw a . . .

_____

- -

_____

- -

_____

Then I saw a . . .

_____

- -

_____

Finally, I saw a . . .

_____

- -

_____

- -

_____

Highlights™

Congratulations!

(your name)

worked hard
and finished the

Writing

Learning Fun Workbook

KINDERGARTEN

Answers

Page 9
Head to Toe

Page 11
Under the Rainbow

Page 13
Clowning Around

Page 15
Silly Garden

8 apples

5 orange carrots

3 birdhouses

1 pair of sunglasses

2 squirrels

7 lollipops in a tree

4 people

Page 17
Sled Ahead!

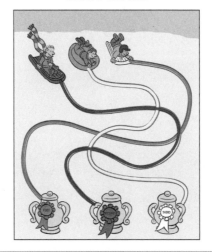

Page 19
Monkey See

Page 21
A Good Day

Page 23
Barnyard Bagpipes

Page 25
Lizzy's Busy Week

Answers

Page 27
On the Job

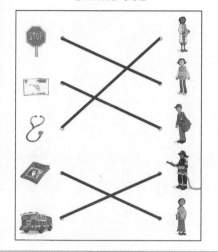

Page 29
Puppet Show

Page 33
Where Is Max's Hat?

Page 35
Sweet Treats

Page 37
Down Under

Page 39
Superhero Party

Page 43
Make a Castle

Inside Back Cover
Scavenger Hunt

A. Page 27
B. Page 15
C. Page 31
D. Page 4
E. Page 17
F. Page 13